What's MIDI?

By
Jon F.
Eiche

**Making musical instruments
work together.**

First printing: September, 1990
Second printing: August, 1991

Eiche, Jon F.
    What's MIDI?: making musical instruments work
together/Jon F. Eiche.
    p. cm.
    Includes index.
    ISBN 0-7935-0082-6 $5.95
    1. MIDI (Standard)   I. Title.
ML1093.E35   1990
786.7'6 – dc20

7777 West Bluemound Road
P.O. Box 13819 Milwaukee, WI 53213

Contents

Introduction 5

1: MIDI in a Nutshell 7

2: What MIDI Does 14

3: (Inter)Facing the Music 28

4: All Systems Go! 37

5: A MIDI Road Map 42

6: Beyond the Notes 48

7: When Trouble Strikes 53

Grand Finale 58

About the Author 59

Index 60

Introduction

COMPLETE THE FOLLOWING SENTENCE:

MIDI is...

A. a code word used by the French resistance during World War I.

B. the call letters of a radio station on the island of Cyprus.

C. a measurement somewhere between MINI and MAXI.

D. one of the most exciting things to happen to music since little Adolphe Sax put his dad's clarinet mouthpiece on his mom's vacuum cleaner.

If you said that the answer is D, give yourself a pat on the back; you already know a little about MIDI, and by reading this book you're assured of learning more.

On the other hand, if you guessed A, B, or C, don't give up hope. Everybody has to start somewhere, and the beginning is the best place of all. Perhaps you're even better off than the "D" people, because you can approach MIDI without prejudice or preconceptions—once we clear up a few details about measurements, radio stations, and World War I.

You see, this MIDI thing has acquired something of an undeserved reputation among musicians and others. It is perceived as something difficult to understand, mysterious, meant only for synthesizer wizards and computer programmers. And yes, it does look like a secret password.

But in reality, using MIDI is as simple as tying your shoes—maybe simpler, since it can be used by people with no manual dexterity whatever.

Best of all, the most important parts of what you need to know about MIDI are right here in this book.

So if you're contemplating a plunge in the waters of MIDI, but you're not sure if they're over your head, remember the three rules of swimming:

1. *Use the buddy system.* Keep this book at your side; it will hold your hand and help you along.

2. *Don't panic.* It's not as threatening as it looks. If all else fails, relax and you'll float.

3. *Wait an hour after eating, so you don't get cramps.* I'm not sure that this really applies to MIDI, but it couldn't hurt.

Let's get started.

1

MIDI in a Nutshell

EXACTLY WHAT *IS* MIDI? If you ask just about anyone who owns an electronic musical instrument that was made since 1984 or so, the answer you'll get is likely to be, "It's those plugs on the back." And that answer is right, as far as it goes.

But the important thing about MIDI is not the physical connectors or the electronics behind it; the important thing is what it allows you to do. For example, with MIDI you can...

- play two instruments from the keyboard of one; or

- record your music for playback later; or

- synchronize the performance of such a recording with that of an automatic drummer.

Still, before you can appreciate all that MIDI does, you really should spend a little time becoming familiar with what it is.

WHAT MIDI IS

The name "MIDI" stands for "Musical Instrument Digital Interface"—quite a mouthful. But by breaking this name down into its component parts, you'll find that it's really pretty easy to understand:

- "Musical Instrument." You already know what that is. MIDI was designed for use in playing music. Over the years it has found other uses, and has been incorporated into pieces of equipment that are not strictly instruments; but "musical instrument" still describes where it is used most often. (Judging by the first paragraph of this chapter, you might think that a more accurate name might be *Electronic* Musical Instrument..." But as you'll see later in this book, MIDI can work for *all* instruments, and voices, too.)

- "Digital." This isn't so difficult. It simply means that computers are involved. Since computers work with numbers, and another word for "numbers" is "digits," the adjective "digital" means that somewhere in that MIDI stuff is a computer of some kind. Now, you don't have to know a thing about computers to enjoy the wonders of MIDI. It's like automobiles: You don't have to be a mechanic to drive a car. So don't let this word scare you.

- "Interface." Uh-oh...this one looks imposing. But the meaning is simple: communication. That's all.

Now that you understand the parts, let's put them back together: Musical instruments communicating with the help of computers. I told you it was easy.

By the way, "MIDI" rhymes more or less with "city." Please don't say "my-dye" unless you want to be branded a "MIDIot."

Time for a history lesson: MIDI is a specification that was developed in the early 1980s to allow musical instruments of different brands to "talk" to one another. It was developed jointly by the major manufacturers of electronic musical instruments, and as such, represents a cooperative effort of impressive proportions. Moreover, that cooperation continues, for MIDI is not a formal standard that must be adhered to; rather, it is a specification that is followed voluntarily by the individual manufacturers.

The MIDI specification consists of two parts:

- The hardware by which MIDI devices are connected.

- The "language" that is "spoken" when the devices "talk" to one another.

Let's look at these parts one at a time.

MIDI HARDWARE

Remember the "plugs" on the back of the instrument? In MIDI jargon these are known as *ports*. There are three possible kinds: In, Out, and Thru.

IN   OUT   THRU

MIDI ports.

- IN receives MIDI information from other equipment.

- OUT sends MIDI information to other equipment.

- THRU provides a duplicate of the information received by IN, to be passed along to other equipment.

Not all MIDI equipment has all three ports, and some devices may have more than one of a given type.

The MIDI ports of different pieces of equipment are connected by special MIDI cables, which have five pins in each end and plug into the ports themselves.

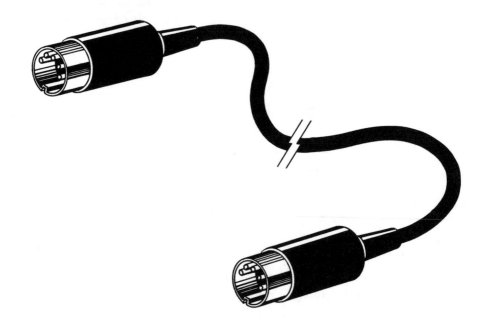

MIDI cable.

We'll look closer at the possible kinds of MIDI connections a little later. But first you should understand a little about what travels through a MIDI cable from one device to another.

THE MIDI LANGUAGE

A MIDI cable is something like a telephone line, in that it allows communication between two points. That communication takes the form of MIDI *messages*.

MIDI RULE #1:

What travels through the MIDI cable is NOT sound; it's information (data).

A typical MIDI instrument will have some kind of audio output, whether it consists of built-in speakers or jacks for connection to external amplification; this audio output is necessary for you to hear the sound that the instrument produces. The MIDI connections are totally separate and different from the audio output. This distinction will be discussed at greater length in Chapter 2.

The information in a MIDI message consists of numbers (remember: *digital* interface). In computer jargon, these numbers are known as *bytes*, but you can think of them as *words*. A typical MIDI message consists of one or more words, the meaning of which is specified in the MIDI language.

It should be mentioned here that not all MIDI devices understand all MIDI messages. While this might seem like a bad thing, it's really not. It's just that MIDI devices tend to be "specialists," and not all areas of the language apply to all devices. For example, there are some messages that pertain to the synchronization of MIDI recording and playback equipment that do not apply to instruments without those functions. It's like a plumber speaking to a chemist; they both speak the same language, but there are some words that are limited to their respective specialties.

The difference is that MIDI devices are "dumb" and totally lacking in curiosity. So when a message comes along that a MIDI device doesn't understand, rather than asking, "What do you mean?" the device will just ignore it and keep going about its own business. This keeps things simple and prevents all kinds of traffic jams in the MIDI cable.

MIDI RULE #2:

MIDI can't make an instrument do something it wasn't designed to do.

So many "problems" with MIDI stem from ignorance of this simple fact. For example, don't expect that connecting a keyboard to a drum machine and holding the keys down will make the drum sounds sustain.

A typical MIDI message consists of two or three words (bytes):

- First is a *status byte*, which tells what kind of message it is. A typical example is the Note On message, which is transmitted when a note is played. The status byte says, "This is a Note On message."

- Next come one or two *data bytes*, which provide further information to complete the message. The Note On message has two data bytes: one to tell which note has been played and one to tell how hard it was struck.

The three words of a typical Note On message could be translated as: "This is a Note On message." "It's for G above middle C." "Play it medium loud." As you can see, MIDI is a lot more succinct than English, requiring only three words to say what took three sentences to describe here. And it is also fast. A complete MIDI message such as the one just described is transmitted in less than a *thousandth* of a second. This means not only that receiving instruments will get messages quickly, but also that many messages can be transmitted in a short time. This is especially useful because MIDI can transmit only one message at a time. For example, if you play a three-note chord on a MIDI keyboard, the three Note On messages are actually sent one after another, in rapid succession.

Two Categories of Messages

MIDI messages are divided into two broad categories: *channel* messages and *system* messages.

- Channel messages are transmitted and received on a specific MIDI channel, which can be compared to a TV channel: An instrument has to be "tuned" to the correct one or it won't receive what is being transmitted. There are 16 channels available, and each one can carry different messages than the others, over the same MIDI cable. This makes it possible, for example, to play different musical parts at the same time.

  There are generally two channel settings that apply to a MIDI instrument: the *transmit channel* is the channel over which an instrument transmits MIDI messages, and the *receive channel* is the channel over which an instrument will respond to MIDI messages that it receives.

- System messages are not restricted to a specific MIDI channel, but rather are transmitted to all equipment that is connected in a MIDI system. This is an efficient way to transmit pertinent information to many instruments at once.

Chapters 3 and 4 will explore channel and system messages in greater depth; but first, an overview of what MIDI can do.

2

What MIDI Does

MIDI CAN BE USED for a lot of different purposes, but the two most common are live performance and recording.

PERFORMANCE

It's been a long time since every movie theater had a pipe organ, as they did during the golden age of silent films. Nowadays such theater organs are found most often in pizza parlors. If you have ever seen one being played, you know what remarkable instruments they are. The organist plays on several rows of keyboards, sending shimmering clouds of sound from the ranks of pipes. Then he reaches over and flips a switch, and suddenly, suspended from the ceiling, a xylophone is playing along with him. He flips another switch and a piano standing against the wall joins in, its keys seemingly being pressed by the fingers of some invisible virtuoso.

The remote control over xylophones, pianos, bells, and drums that is within the power of the theater organ makes it seem to be a magical instrument indeed. It is precisely this kind of remote control that the authors of the MIDI specification had in mind when they designed MIDI.

The theater organ: a pre-MIDI music system.

The simplest kind of MIDI setup is playing two instruments from one keyboard. This is called a "master-slave" connection. In this case, the instrument whose keyboard you wish to play (the master) should have a MIDI cable connected to its MIDI OUT port. The other end of the cable should plug into the MIDI IN port on the other instrument (the slave).

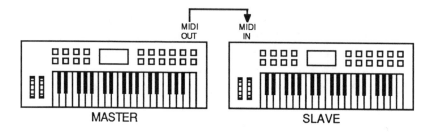

A master-slave connection.

Now when you play the keyboard of the master, the slave will sound as well. When you play, the master transmits messages through the MIDI cable—messages that are received by the slave, which responds as if its own keyboard were being played. The only difference is that the keys themselves don't actually move. This doubling of parts by MIDI control is sometimes called *layering*, or *stacking*, sounds.

If you connect IN to OUT, rather than OUT to IN, the other instrument becomes the master. If you use two cables, connecting IN to OUT and OUT to IN, you can use either instrument as the master.

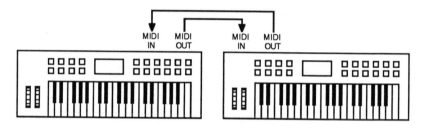

A two-way master-slave connection.

It is important to reemphasize that what is being sent over the MIDI cable is information, not sound. The sound being produced by the slave (piano, strings, quacking ducks, etc.) is not dependent on the sound produced by the master. In fact, the usefulness of this kind of setup lies in having each instrument produce a different sound, resulting in a doubling of parts analogous to different sections of an orchestra playing the same notes. Furthermore, the master and the slave both require some sort of audio output; the MIDI connection does not eliminate the need for both instruments to be connected to amplification and loudspeakers in order to be heard.

Because a slave can be played without its own keyboard being touched, instruments are now made for the express purpose of being MIDI slaves. These instruments, called *tone modules*, or *expander modules*, have no keyboards of their own, and thus cost less than comparable instruments that have keyboards.

Such modules are frequently made to be mounted in standard-size equipment racks; these *rack-mount* units save not only money, but also space. Tone modules rely on incoming MIDI messages to play them.

The flip side of the coin is the MIDI *master controller*. Such "instruments" produce no sound of their own, but are made solely to transmit MIDI messages to slaves. Keyboards are the most common controllers, but there are also wind controllers (for woodwind and brass players), percussion controllers (for drummers and mallet players), and guitar controllers (some of these can be played as regular guitars, too). There are even *pitch-to-MIDI converters*, which allow an acoustic instrument—or even the human voice—to be used as a MIDI controller.

No matter what kinds of devices the master and slave are—synthesizers, tone modules, portable keyboards, etc.—human nature dictates that you will want to add more of them to your MIDI setup sooner or later. The MIDI THRU port allows such additions to be made. Adding slaves in series in this way is known as *daisy-chaining*.

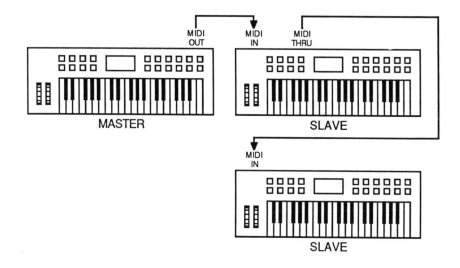

A simple daisy-chain setup.

Messages are transmitted by the MIDI OUT port of the master and received by the MIDI IN port of the first slave. These messages are passed along to the MIDI THRU port of this slave, which is connected to the MIDI IN port of the following slave. This allows the messages to reach all of the instruments.

There are a few aspects of such a setup that may not be apparent on the surface:

- Every instrument needs its own audio output. For instruments with built-in speakers, those outputs are already provided. But for instruments without them, external amplification is required. Even a small MIDI setup may need a *mixer*—a device that mixes together audio signals from several sources (in this case, musical instruments). The output of the mixer is fed to a power amplifier, which drives one or more loudspeakers.

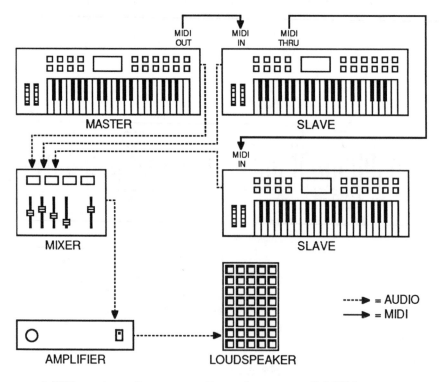

MIDI and audio connections for a small MIDI setup.

You may be tempted to use a "Y" cord to mix audio signals; don't. This distorts the audio signals.

- If you have an instrument of a certain type or brand that you like, you may be tempted to buy another like it. As a rule, your money is better spent on one that sounds different, both to give you a greater variety of sounds and to increase the likelihood that your instruments will complement, rather than merely duplicate, one another. And after all, MIDI was designed to allow different brands of equipment to be used together.

- There is a potential problem in daisy-chaining more than two or three slaves: Transmission can become unreliable. The solution is to use a MIDI THRU box, which produces several THRU signals from one IN.

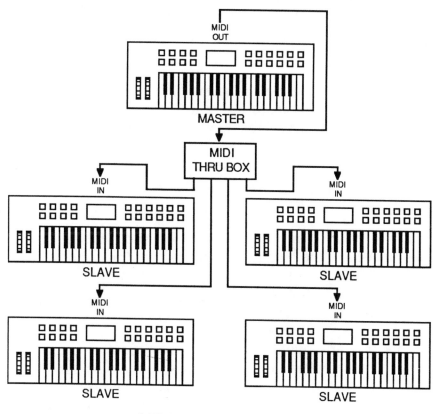

MIDI THRU box in use.

Such a system is known as a *star* setup, because the MIDI cables connected to the THRU box resemble the points of a star.

The use of a large number of slaves is encountered less frequently in live performance (except onstage in a big rock group) than it is in MIDI recording and playback. Let's look at that next.

MIDI RECORDING AND PLAYBACK (SEQUENCING)

There used to be a law that stated that all electronic musical instruments had to begin with the letter "s." This law has since been repealed on the grounds that it violated the rights of the other letters, but it has left us with a legacy of synthesizers, samplers, and sequencers. *Sequencer,* or *sequence recorder,* is the name by which MIDI recorders are still sometimes known. Consequently, using one of these devices is known as *sequencing.*

A sequencer can either be a separate "box" that is designed for the purpose of MIDI recording, or a feature built into an instrument such as a portable keyboard or synthesizer, or a software program running on a general-purpose computer. No matter what form a sequencer takes, and no matter what "bells and whistles" (special features) it may have, all sequencers perform the same basic task.

You can think of it simply as recording. And it is similar in many respects to the tape recording that you probably are familiar with: Set the recorder to RECORD and play into it; it records what you play. Press STOP, then PLAY; it plays it back what you recorded. But there are some differences.

First, notice that sequence recorders don't require you to rewind the tape before you can play back what you recorded. This is because there is no tape involved! The recording takes place in computer memory, so you don't have to wait for it to rewind.

20

Second, sequencers record MIDI messages, NOT sound. What's being stored in memory are Note On, Note Off, and other such messages (more about which in Chapters 3 and 4). This makes possible a number of things that are totally beyond the capabilities of tape recorders:

- You can play back the music with a different sound than you used during recording.

- You can change the speed (tempo) of the playback to something different than the speed at which you recorded, without changing the pitch of the music.

- You can enter notes one at a time (*step-time* recording), rather than playing in tempo (*real-time* recording).

- You can edit what you have recorded. Examples that are possible on many sequencers include the ability to "straighten out" imprecise rhythms (*quantization*) and the ability to change the pitch of a single wrong note (*event editing*).

Perhaps a closer analogy than the tape recorder is the player piano. You remember those, don't you? Music is stored on a roll of paper with holes punched in it. The paper is drawn through the player piano, and the positions and lengths of the holes determine what notes play and how long they are held. Like the MIDI sequence recorder, the piano roll records and plays back *performance information*, rather than the sound itself. So the recording can be slowed down, sped up, played back on a different instrument, and so on, in ways that tape recordings can't.

21

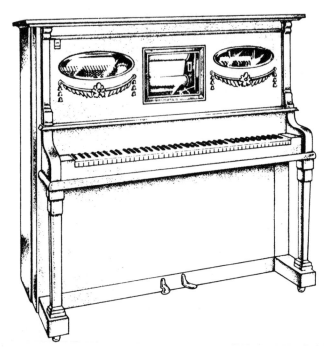

The player piano: an early (non-MIDI) sequencer.

The MIDI connections for a basic sequencing setup are simple:
OUT to IN, IN to OUT.

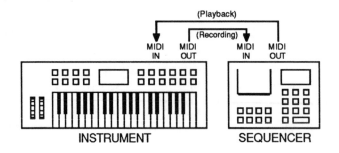

A basic sequencing setup.

When the sequencer records, you play the instrument. What
you play is transmitted, as MIDI messages, out the MIDI OUT
port on the instrument, through a MIDI cable, and into the
MIDI IN port on the sequencer.

When the sequencer plays back your recording, *it* plays the instrument. The recording is transmitted out the MIDI OUT port on the sequencer, through a MIDI cable, into the MIDI IN port on the instrument.

Things become more interesting when you add instruments to the setup. For example, you now need to be concerned with recording on different MIDI channels. This is generally handled in one of three ways:

- You change the *transmit channel* on the master instrument for every new part you record. OR

- You change the *record channel assignment* on the sequencer for every new part you record. OR

- You set the *playback channel assignment* on the sequencer for every part that the sequencer plays back.

The option that you use depends on what your equipment can do. Some instruments don't allow you to change the transmit channel; some sequencers don't have the ability to assign MIDI messages to a specific channel.

If you lack all of these capabilities, you can accomplish the same thing by using a device called a *MIDI channelizer*. With this device, you can cause the messages transmitted by the master to be assigned to whatever channel you wish.

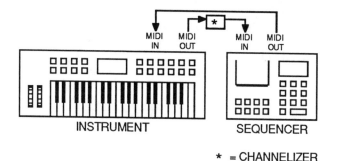

* = CHANNELIZER

Placement of a MIDI channelizer.

23

More and more instruments are being made that are *multitimbral*—capable of playing several different sounds at one time. Many of these instruments either have sequencers built in or have optional external sequencers available that are designed to work well with them. With many of these instruments, you don't even have to know about MIDI channels; you simply record different parts, one after the other, choosing the sounds you desire. The sequencer is "smart" enough to select the appropriate MIDI channels for you. The adjective "user-friendly" is widely abused, but in this case it seems to fit!

Control over the flow of MIDI information becomes more involved when you have more than one instrument. For example, look at the following illustration of a reasonably simple MIDI system, consisting of a master, a slave, and a sequencer:

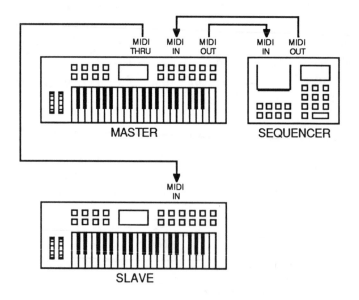

A sequencing setup with two instruments.

In order for such a setup to work best, so that the appropriate instruments sound both during recording and during playback, two things are required:

- The sequencer should employ a function known as *soft thru*, *patch thru*, or *echo back*. Normally, the MIDI OUT port of a sequencer only transmits what is recorded in the memory of the sequencer. But when soft thru is on, the OUT port also acts as a THRU port, passing along what is received by the IN port. (It's like the commercial: "It's a floor wax AND a dessert topping.")

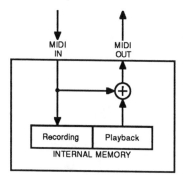

Soft thru on.

If the sequencer doesn't have soft thru, a *MIDI merger* can accomplish the same thing by combining the outputs of the sequencer's OUT and THRU ports. (Never, NEVER use a "Y" cord for this purpose. It's a bad idea for audio mixing and a worse one for MIDI.)

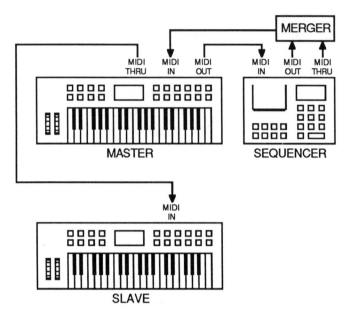

MIDI merger as an alternative to soft thru.

- The master instrument should employ a capability known as *local control off*. Local control has to do with whether or not an instrument plays itself—for example, whether the keyboard of a synthesizer causes the sound-producing circuitry of the synthesizer to play.

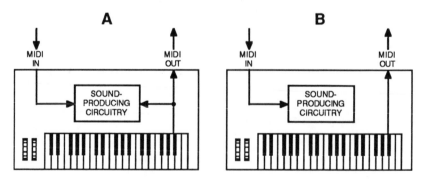

Local control on (A), off (B).

When local control is off, playing the master doesn't produce a sound directly. Rather, the MIDI messages transmitted from the master to the sequencer, and returned to the master via the soft thru, are what cause the master to sound. This avoids problems with doubled notes that would occur during recording if local control were on.

Returning to the illustration on page 24: When the sequencer employs soft thru (or a MIDI merger) and the master employs local control off, MIDI messages can reach both the master and the slave during recording and playback alike.

- During recording, messages go out the OUT of the master, in the IN of the sequencer (where they are recorded), thru the sequencer, in the IN of the master, thru the master, and in the IN of the slave.

- During playback, messages go out the OUT of the sequencer, in the IN of the master, thru the master, and in the IN of the slave.

In both cases, messages reach both the master and the slave. The receive channels that are set on the instruments determine what messages they respond to and what messages they ignore.

For more information about MIDI sequencers and sequencing, see *What's a Sequencer?* by Greg R. Starr (Hal Leonard Publishing, 1990).

3

(Inter)Facing the Music

IT'S TIME TO LOOK more closely at the information that travels through the MIDI cable. This chapter briefly explains the various channel messages, and the next does the same thing for the system messages.

The status byte of every channel message—the first "word" of the message, which identifies what kind of message it is—includes the channel on which that message is being transmitted. To return to our familiar example of Note On, the status byte doesn't merely say, "This is a Note On message"; it says, "This is a Note On message on Channel X," where "X" can be any number from 1 through 16.

This inclusion of the channel number within the message makes it possible to send messages on multiple channels through a single MIDI cable. The receiving instrument responds only to the channel(s) for which it is set, and ignores the rest.

Channel messages are divided into two subcategories:

- Channel *voice* messages, which are where most of the MIDI action takes place. These are the messages that convey the information about a performance—like the holes in the piano roll.

- Channel *mode* messages, which have to do with how an instrument responds to channel voice messages. This will be clarified shortly.

CHANNEL VOICE MESSAGES

Note On. This message seems like an old friend already. It means to start a note.

Thε status byte says, "Note On on Channel X."

The first data byte says what note to start. Remember that MIDI is a *digital* interface, so everything is specified by numbers. There are 128 MIDI note numbers from which to choose (0–127). To give you an idea of how wide a spread of notes this is, the 88 notes of the piano keyboard correspond to MIDI note numbers 21–108. Middle C is note number 60. (MIDI says nothing about the actual pitch produced by an instrument—merely the note number. This independence of note number and pitch is one of the things that makes MIDI instruments so flexible.)

The second data byte says at what velocity (how hard; literally, how fast) the note is played. Although most MIDI instruments translate velocity into loudness (the higher the velocity, the louder the note—like on a piano), an instrument might be able to do other things with this information (for example, play notes *softer* with higher velocities).

29

The range of velocities is 1–127. (You'll find that 127 and 128 are "magic numbers" in MIDI. The reason has to do with technical details of MIDI mathematics that you needn't be concerned with.) An instrument that is not *velocity-sensitive* transmits all notes with the same velocity—64 on most such instruments, since it is essentially midway between 1 and 127. Some instruments that can't send different velocities from their own keyboards *can* respond to different velocities via MIDI; this is common in budget instruments.

A special aspect of this message is that a Note On with a velocity of 0 acts as a Note Off—it silences the note number that is specified in the first data byte. Instruments that transmit Note-On-with-0-velocity instead of the discrete Note Off message (described next) usually use something called *running status* to reduce the number of bytes that must be transmitted.

Running status is a special MIDI rule that states that, for multiple channel messages with the same status byte (e.g., Note On on Channel 1), the status byte need only be transmitted once, at the beginning of the group of messages.

Note Off. Note off is the complement of Note On; it is used to stop a note.

The status byte says "This is a Note Off message on Channel X."

The first data byte tells what note number is to be turned off.

The second data byte is a velocity value, corresponding to how fast the key is released on a keyboard instrument. Not many instruments transmit or respond to release velocity, as it's known. Since some velocity value must be present in the message, the velocity is generally set at 64 and ignored. Consequently, the Note Off message has little practical advantage over the Note On with a velocity of 0.

In most circumstances, it makes no difference whether your instruments use the separate Note Off message or not.

Pressure (After-Touch). Some keyboards have the ability to respond to pressure on the keys after the notes have been played. For those that do, Pressure is the message that is usually transmitted. (Non-keyboard MIDI instruments often transmit Pressure messages in different ways. MIDI guitars usually use a variable pedal; MIDI wind instruments usually use breath pressure.)

Actually, Pressure is not one message, but two distinct ones:

- *Channel (monophonic)* Pressure is transmitted no matter what key is pressed, and it affects all notes playing on that channel.

- *Key (polyphonic)* Pressure is transmitted separately for each key, and it affects only the note number for which it is transmitted. It is more versatile than channel pressure, but it can easily "clog up" the MIDI cable with an abundance of messages. It is also more expensive to implement than channel pressure. Consequently it is the less common of the two.

Many instruments (especially inexpensive ones) do not transmit or respond to any pressure messages. Others implement only channel pressure. A small number allow both channel pressure and key pressure—though usually not at the same time.

Control Change. The people who designed MIDI were not merely a collection of cold, unfeeling engineers. On the contrary, they were dyed-in-the-wool *romantics*, who remembered with misty-eyed fondness the bygone days when the control panel of a typical synthesizer was festooned with knobs and switches galore, and that by using those knobs and switches, it was possible to manipulate the sound in exciting ways during performance. They remembered, and they reasoned that MIDI ought to provide something like that kind of control for newer instruments.

So they designated a separate set of channel voice messages as Control Change messages. You can think of them as MIDI knobs and switches.

There are 128 possible MIDI controller numbers available (0–127).

- Numbers 0–31 are *continuous* controllers; they're the MIDI "knobs," although they may take the physical form of sliders, wheels, variable pedals, breath controllers, etc.

- Numbers 64–95 are *on/off* controllers; they're the MIDI "switches," and they are often buttons or pedals.

These are the most important numbers; don't worry about the others.

Of these controllers, some have specific definitions. For example:

CONTROLLER #	DEFINITION
1	Modulation Controller
2	Breath Controller
7	Volume
64	Sustain Pedal

Some MIDI instruments allow you to decide what MIDI controller number will be assigned to a given physical controller. This flexible assignment, called controller *mapping*, can be useful in making two instruments work well together.

Program Change (Patch Select). Most MIDI instruments offer more than one sound for you to play. Such sounds are often called *programs*, or *patches*. As a rule, selecting a program on a MIDI instrument will cause that instrument to transmit a Program Change message. This way, for example, any slave units can change programs, too. Or the program number can be recorded at the beginning of a sequencer recording, so that upon playback the same program number is always selected.

Notice that it is the *number* of the program that is transmitted—not the sound itself. When you select program number 5, it may be Piccolo on the master instrument and Foghorn on the slave. And if you have a synthesizer and decide to change program 8 from a Violin sound to a Gong, watch out when you play back the sequence that has a Program Change 8 message recorded at the beginning.

Program numbering is always fun to try to figure out. The MIDI Program Change message can use the numbers 0–127. But the buttons on the instrument may be numbered starting with 0, or 1, or 11, or possibly something else. You can thank the people who design instruments this way, because they help to keep the writers of owner's manuals employed.

Just as some instruments allow you to *map* the physical controllers to different MIDI controller numbers, some allow you to map the sounds to different MIDI program numbers. Depending on the instrument, either the program numbers transmitted, or those received, or both, may be mapped. This is helpful when you want something other than Foghorn to pop up on the slave when you choose Piccolo on the master. But it can also cause confusion: Imagine choosing program number 3, but it is mapped to transmit number 17 instead; and when the slave receives 17, it is mapped to select 84 instead!

Pitch Bend. The Pitch Bend messages do what they say: They bend the pitch up or down from whatever the "normal" pitch is. On keyboards, a special wheel, lever, or joy stick near the left end of the keyboard is often responsible for pitch bend.

As with MIDI note numbers, Pitch Bend messages do not concern themselves with the actual pitch involved. A message of, say, "Bend the pitch up 100" might result in a different amount of pitch change on two different instruments, depending on the *pitch bend range* of each instrument. This range setting, which may or may not be programmable (changeable) on your instruments, determines how far up or down the pitch will actually bend when it receives the highest or lowest possible Pitch Bend message. If the pitch bend range is set to 12 half steps, for example, the highest Pitch Bend value will bend the pitch up one octave (12 half steps); the lowest value will bend the pitch down by the same amount. (NOTE: Some instruments have separately definable upward and downward pitch bend ranges.)

Pitch Bend, continuous controllers, and Pressure are called *continuous messages*—often transmitted in long streams to reflect the changing position of the physical controller involved.

CHANNEL MODE MESSAGES

MIDI modes, as mentioned earlier, have to do with how an instrument responds to channel voice messages. There are two aspects to this response:

- Omni Off or Omni On. When Omni is Off, the receiving instrument has to be "tuned" to a particular channel in order to respond to channel voice messages on that channel. This is how channels were explained a couple of chapters ago. But wait! There's more! When Omni is On, it means that the instrument responds to channel voice messages on all channels ("Omni" means "all").

  Remember that the status byte of a channel voice message includes the number of the channel. With Omni Off, the receiving instrument pays attention to that channel information; with Omni On, it disregards the channel information and responds to all channels.

  Notice that the Omni setting, like the other mode settings, has to do with reception of MIDI messages, not transmission. Nothing transmits with Omni On.

- Poly or Mono. When Poly is On, the instrument can play more than one note at a time (polyphonic response). When Mono is On, the instrument plays only one note at a time (monophonic response).

These two aspects of MIDI response can be combined in four different ways, and these are the four MIDI modes:

- Mode 1: Omni On, Poly. The instrument responds to all channels and plays polyphonically. Sometimes called Omni mode.

- Mode 2: Omni On, Mono. The instrument responds to all channels and plays monophonically.

- Mode 3: Omni Off, Poly. The instrument responds to only one channel at a time and plays polyphonically. Sometimes called Poly mode.

- Mode 4: Omni Off, Mono. The instrument responds to several adjacent channels and plays monophonically on each of these. Sometimes called Mono mode.

Mode 2 is rarely used. Modes 1 and 3 are common among instruments that can play one sound at a time. Mode 4 is used in *multitimbral* instruments—those that can play more than one sound at a time, on different MIDI channels. In fact, most Mode 4 instruments actually respond polyphonically on the various channels; this is known as *multi* mode, although it is not an official MIDI mode.

These are the modes, and all receiving instruments employ at least one of them. The mode *messages* give the ability for the mode to be set remotely, via MIDI.

There are messages to turn Omni Off, Omni On, Poly On, and Mono On. The Mono On message includes the ability to determine how many adjacent channels the instrument will respond to.

If you're particularly astute, you might ask the question, "If an instrument can respond to more than one MIDI channel at a time, on what channel are the channel mode messages transmitted?" The answer is that within the instrument itself there will be a setting (which you may or may not be able to change, depending on the instrument) designating one channel as the *Basic* channel. This is the channel over which the instrument responds to mode messages; it is also the first of the adjacent channels used in Mono mode.

An additional channel designation found in some multitimbral instruments is the *Global* channel. It is defined as the Basic channel minus 1 (or, if the Basic channel is 1, channel 16). It is used for messages intended to affect all parts, such as Pressure.

In addition to the messages that actually set the mode, channel mode messages include a couple of related items:

- Local Control On/Off. This is used to determine whether the playing mechanism of an instrument (e.g., the keyboard) is internally connected to the sound-producing circuitry. Chapter 2 discussed the use of local control off in sequencing. Be aware that whether or not an instrument responds to local control messages is a separate matter from whether or not local control can be set from the panel of the instrument.

- All Notes Off. This is used to silence all notes on a given channel. MIDI devices that employ a "panic button" to cut off stuck notes usually use this message. (Some instruments transmit this message every time all of the keys are released on the keyboard; this is not the use for which the message was intended, and it can result in notes being chopped short during sequencing.)

The channel mode messages are actually part of the Control Change category of channel voice messages. To be specific, they are controller numbers 122-127. Except for the Local Control message (number 122), every mode message is supposed to function as an All Notes Off message; this way, there should be no possibility of notes becoming stuck when an instrument changes modes.

4

All Systems Go!

WHILE CHANNEL MESSAGES are transmitted on a specific MIDI channel, system messages do not have this restriction. This allows them to communicate certain kinds of information to an entire MIDI system.

System messages are divided into three subcategories:

- System *real-time* messages, which have to do with synchronization of devices such as sequencers and drum machines.

- System *common* messages, which cover miscellaneous functions.

- System *exclusive* messages, which are primarily concerned with information that is exclusive to a certain brand or model of instrument.

SYSTEM REAL-TIME MESSAGES

Picture, if you will, the following scene: A humble music hobbyist, Norman Neophyte by name, has just bought a MIDI drum machine to provide a beat for his compositional endeavors. His previous purchases include a sequencer and assorted MIDI keyboards. He brings his shiny new toy home from the store, takes it out of the box, and connects the MIDI cables. Slowly he reaches for the START button. Unknown to him, Mr. Neophyte is about to cross over into...The Timing Zone.

Whenever you have two pieces of equipment that produce a timed sequence of events, you need a way to synchronize them. The most common occurrence of this is the combination of sequencer and drum machine, but arpeggiators, MIDI delay devices, and multiple sequencers are other possibilities.

System real-time messages provide that synchronization. There are messages to Start and Stop recording or playback, so that devices begin and end at the same time. There is also a Continue message, for resuming playback at the point it was last stopped.

Most importantly, there is the MIDI Timing Clock message, which is transmitted 24 times during every quarter note, to keep things in sync.

In order for this synchronization to work, one device is designated as the master and any others are made the slaves. The master is set to use its *internal* clock as its timing reference. It transmits real-time messages from its MIDI OUT port to any slaves, which receive these messages via their MIDI IN ports. The slaves are set to use the *external (MIDI)* clock as their timing reference, so that they stay with the master.

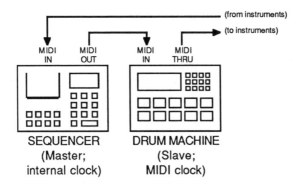

(from instruments)
(to instruments)

MIDI IN | MIDI OUT | MIDI IN | MIDI THRU

SEQUENCER
(Master;
internal clock)

DRUM MACHINE
(Slave;
MIDI clock)

One example of connections for synchronization.

Other system real-time messages are:

- Active Sensing. This is transmitted several times a second by some equipment (synthesizers, especially) as a way of notifying connected units that "I'm still here." The idea is that if the MIDI cable is accidentally disconnected, the receiving unit will realize it because it has stopped receiving Active Sensing messages. The unit can then act to silence any stuck notes that may have resulted from the disconnection.

- System Reset. This message can theoretically be used (in reality, not many devices employ it) to reset all equipment in the system—another "panic button" type of command.

Since timing is crucial for system real-time messages to do their jobs, they are all one-byte messages. This means they can communicate the necessary information in the least possible amount of time.

Furthermore, they may appear whenever necessary in the MIDI data stream—even in the middle of another message. This assures that accurate timing can be maintained.

SYSTEM COMMON MESSAGES

The category of system common messages is a catch-all for functions that don't fit anywhere else:

- Song Position Pointer. This message allows sequencers and drum machines to align themselves to the same place within a song. Once the location within the song is established, a real-time Continue message can be used to begin recording or playback from that point.

- Song Select. Some sequencers and drum machines can store more than one song in memory at a time. This message allows the correct song number to be chosen from among those available.

- Tune Request. This message is used with analog synthesizers, to request them to tune their oscillators. I'll try to refrain from waxing poetic about how wonderful the old analog synths are when compared to the newer digital ones. Suffice it to say that few instruments use this message any more.

An addendum to the original MIDI specification, called MIDI Time Code (MTC), also makes use of system common messages. MTC is a system of synchronizing MIDI with the real world. Whereas MIDI real-time messages provide a system of *relative* time (24 clocks per quarter note; the quarter note itself can be fast or slow), MTC runs on *absolute* time (hours, minutes, seconds, and fractions of seconds). This is especially important in the synchronization of sound to film and video.

The one MTC message incorporated into the system common category is the Quarter Frame message. This is more or less analogous to the MIDI Timing Clock, except that it contains references to the current absolute time.

The rest of the MTC messages are in the system exclusive category.

System Exclusive Messages

The idea behind MIDI is communication between instruments of any brand. But the designers of the specification foresaw a need for instruments of a given brand to be able to exchange information that pertained only to that brand or model. System exclusive messages were their answer to that need.

Manufacturers of MIDI equipment are assigned unique ID (identification) numbers for use in their system exclusive messages. Beyond the use of the ID number, there is little that is standardized about the "sys-ex" message, as it is known. The manufacturers are free to use them to communicate whatever, and however much, information they wish.

The most common use is to transmit patch settings (parameters) between instruments, or between an instrument and a computer that is running special software designed to display, manipulate, or store such settings. Often, the entire contents of an instrument's memory can be transmitted in a sys-ex message—something known as a memory *dump*.

Since the system exclusive category was so loosely defined when the MIDI specification was first written, it has been used as a convenient place to make additions to the "spec":

- MIDI Time Code. This was discussed briefly under system common messages. The MTC messages that do the bulk of the work—such as directing a piece of equipment to start or stop recording at a certain point, or to rewind to a specific location—are special system exclusive messages.

- Sample Dump Standard. This is a universal way of transferring sampled (digitally recorded) sounds between MIDI instruments—even those of different brands.

The ID numbers used in these messages identify the specific kind of message, rather than a manufacturer.

41

5

A MIDI Road Map

EARLIER IN THE BOOK it was stated that not all MIDI devices understand all MIDI messages, nor should they. A sequencer may transmit and receive system real-time messages, while a tone module has no need of them. In fact, the tone module may not transmit any MIDI messages at all, and for this reason may not even have a MIDI OUT port.

"Wouldn't it be a good idea," you might be saying, "to have some standardized way of seeing at a glance exactly what parts of the MIDI specification an instrument implements?" The authors of the MIDI spec thought so, too. And so they designed the *MIDI Implementation Chart* (or *imp chart*, as it's known colloquially).

A blank copy of this chart appears on pages 44 and 45. Manufacturers are supposed to provide such a chart (filled in, of course) with every piece of MIDI equipment that they make. It's always the same size and format, so that instruments can be compared easily. (Understand that you can't compare every feature on two instruments this way—only the MIDI messages they implement.)

The top of the chart shows the manufacturer, model, and version number of the instrument, as well as the date of the chart itself.

The body of the chart is divided into four columns: a list of MIDI functions, a column indicating whether those functions are transmitted, one indicating whether they are recognized, and an additional column for any clarifying remarks that the manufacturer considers necessary.

At the bottom of the chart is a space for any additional notes. Below this are definitions of the mode numbers (since the modes are referred to by number within the chart) and a key to the symbols that mean "yes" and "no" in the chart. Usually "o" means "yes" and "x" means "no," but occasionally you'll find the reverse.

That's just about all there is to it. If a function shows the symbol for "yes" in the "Transmitted" column, it means that the device transmits that message. If it shows the symbol for "no" in the "Recognized" column, it means that it doesn't recognize it. Simple, yes? No?

No. It's not quite that simple. For example, recall the tone module without a MIDI OUT port. The "Transmitted" column on the imp chart for this device might have all "x's", or it might have all blanks, or dashes, or it might be filled with "N/A's" (for "Not Applicable").

Or consider an instrument that can be programmed to transmit or not transmit Program Change messages. The appropriate box on the chart might contain "ox", or "?", or "*", or possibly something else. The meaning here will ideally be clarified in the notes or remarks.

MIDI Implementation Chart

Manufacturer: Model:
                                  Version: Date:

Function	Transmitted	Recognized	Remarks
Basic Default			
Channel Changed			
Mode Default			
Messages			
Altered			
Note			
Number : True voice			
Velocity Note ON			
Note OFF			
After Key's			
Touch Ch's			
Pitch Bender			
Control			
Change			

44

```
|                                  |
|Prog                    |         |
|Change : True #         |         |
|                        |         |
|System Exclusive        |         |
|                        |         |
|System : Song Pos       |         |
|       : Song Sel       |         |
|Common : Tune           |         |
|                        |         |
|System :Clock           |         |
|Real Time :Commands     |         |
|                        |         |
|Aux    :Local ON/OFF    |         |
|       :All Notes OFF   |         |
|Mes-   :Active Sense    |         |
|sages:Reset             |         |
|                        |         |
|Notes:                  |         |
```

Mode 1 : OMNI ON, POLY   Mode 2 : OMNI ON, MONO

Mode 3 : OMNI OFF, POLY   Mode 4 : OMNI OFF, MONO

o : Yes

x : No

It's worth taking a moment at this point to cite another MIDI "Rule":

Even if a device implements a MIDI message, it may have to be programmed to transmit it or respond to it.

Fortunately, such "programming" is not at all like computer programming; it usually amounts to merely pressing a few buttons and setting a few controls.

Some functions on the implementation chart call for more than merely a yes-or-no response. Note Number, for example, requires a range of numbers in the appropriate box(es).

Now that you understand how an imp chart "works," let's quickly go through the functions to explain any other potentially puzzling details.

Basic Channel. "Default" means the setting when the unit is first switched on. "Changed" indicates to what channels you can change this setting.

Mode. "Default" is the mode set when the unit is first switched on. "Messages" means channel mode messages transmitted or received. "Altered" applies to the "Recognized" column on some instruments; when these instruments receive a mode message that they don't implement, they alter it to a message that they do recognize.

Note Number. This is the range of MIDI note numbers that the instrument transmits or recognizes. If the range transmitted is larger than the number of keys on the keyboard of the instrument, it usually means that the instrument has a transpose function that allows it access to the additional notes. If two ranges are shown in the "Recognized" column, and the True Voice range is the smaller of the two, it means that note numbers outside the True Voice range are shifted by one or more octaves until they fall within that range.

Velocity. This is mostly self-explanatory. The one odd thing you might see is something like "9nH (v=0)" for Note Off, which means merely that a Note On message with a velocity of 0 is substituted for a Note Off message.

After Touch. Separate entries for Key (polyphonic) and Channel (monophonic) Pressure messages.

Pitch Bender, Control Change. Self-explanatory.

Program Change. The True Number here is similar to the True Voice in the Note Number entry: It indicates whether an instrument substitutes program numbers when it receives numbers outside its range.

System Exclusive. Self-explanatory, but not much help. An instrument that transmits or recognizes sys-ex messages should have a separate document available describing those messages in detail—for those who want to "get their hands dirty" by using sys-ex to communicate with the instrument.

System Common, System Real Time, Auxiliary Messages. Self-explanatory. "Commands" under System Real Time refers to the Start, Stop, and Continue messages.

6

Beyond the Notes

THIS BOOK HAS ALREADY COVERED the most common uses of MIDI (live performance and sequencing), as well as the most common MIDI devices (musical instruments, sequencers, and drum machines). But there's more to the story than that.

MIDI ports appear on an astounding variety of different devices. Some of these are used to enhance the basic applications of performance and sequencing, while others open up new areas of communication. For example:

- MIDI *lighting controllers* are used to tie the changes in lighting for a performance to the changes in the music.

- MIDI *signal processing* (*effects*) devices, such as reverb and delay, change the character of the sound in response to MIDI messages. This gives musicians more precise and elaborate control over such effects than was previously possible.

- MIDI-controlled *mixing* allows intricate changes in balance among several parts to be handled automatically by a MIDI sequencer.

- MIDI *synchronization devices* translate system real-time or MIDI Time Code messages into a form that can be recorded on tape, so that sequencers and tape recorders can be used together.

In addition to these categories, there are *MIDI processors*. These are altogether different from the MIDI-controlled signal processors just mentioned. A signal processor responds to MIDI messages, but acts on the audio signal—the sound. A MIDI processor acts on the MIDI messages themselves—intercepting them, altering or redirecting them, and sending them on their way again.

A MIDI THRU box is a simple MIDI processor. It takes one MIDI OUT and allows it to be directed to several INs. A more elaborate device, known as a *MIDI patch bay*, or *routing box*, accepts several INs and several OUTs. Any of the INs can be directed to any of the OUTs, by means of routings that are programmed in the device and recalled with the touch of a button. This saves having to unplug and replug MIDI cables every time you wish to change which device is "talking" to which.

Mergers and *channelizers*, mentioned in Chapter 2, are also MIDI processors. Another prominent category is MIDI *filters*—which can block a certain kind of message from being passed on. MIDI *delays* can produce a variety of repeating or echo effects, often synchronized to MIDI Timing Clock messages.

Really elaborate processors can *map* (change) one kind of message to another—for example, changing an After Touch message to Pitch Bend. Since MIDI messages are just numbers after all, such mapping devices can do wonders by applying a little basic math—change high numbers to low ones and vice versa, for instance.

But despite the usefulness of all these specialized devices, arguably the most important MIDI device is a general-purpose one: the computer.

THE COMPUTER CONNECTION

The digital messages of MIDI are made to order for personal computers. But two things are necessary in order for a computer to "speak MIDI":

- First, the computer must have MIDI ports. Although a few models have such ports built-in, most require the addition of a *MIDI interface* (that's right: a "Musical Instrument Digital Interface interface") to provide them.

- Second, the computer must have a MIDI *program*—a piece of *software*. A computer, contrary to popular belief, is not "smart"; it is exceedingly stupid. It can't do anything until it is told exactly what to do and how to do it. Software is what tells it.

There are several advantages to using computers for MIDI applications:

- The computer *display* is able to show a great deal of information at a glance. Many MIDI programs possess the further advantage of a *graphical* representation of MIDI messages—points, lines, curves, and other shapes that can be understood easily and can be changed by being "moved around" onscreen.

- The internal *memory* of a computer usually provides ample "space" for information to be kept and manipulated. And external storage, in the form one or more *disk drives*, makes it easy to keep information after working with it, so it can be retrieved quickly.

- Computers are *versatile*; they can perform many different roles, depending on the software that is put into them.

The computer: the ultimate MIDI instrument?

The software that a computer runs determines exactly what use it makes of the MIDI ports it has. There are several kinds of MIDI software available for personal computers:

- **Patch librarians** allow you to assemble a "library" of sounds for your synthesizer. The patches are transferred between synthesizer and computer using system exclusive information.

- **Patch editors,** or **voicing** programs, allow you to edit voices with the help of the computer. Again, sys-ex messages make this possible. Some of these programs go so far as to "invent" new patches for you.

- **Sample editors** are the equivalent of patch editors for sampling instruments. Digitally recorded sounds can be cut, spliced, looped, redrawn, and more. Many such programs use the MIDI Sample Dump Standard to "translate" sampled sounds from one brand or model of sampling instrument to another.

51

- **Drum machine pattern editors** assist you in composing and altering percussion patterns for drum machines.

- **Sequencers** offer capabilities beyond special-purpose hardware sequencers. There are even programs that do some of the composing for you. Increasingly, sequencers store sequences as Standard MIDI Files, a format developed to allow the same music to be recorded, played back, and edited by different sequencers.

- **Song albums** are arrangements of music. The advantage of these over conventional recordings is the same as that of other sequences: the ability to change anything about the performance (tempo, sounds, number of parts, etc.).

- **Music printing (scoring)** programs give you "sheet music" from the computer printer. Sometimes these are combined with a software sequencer.

- **Telecommunications** programs allow you to send and receive MIDI information over the phone.

- **Education** programs cover all aspects of music, from basic notation to ear training to playing technique.

- **Digital recording** programs offer the computer counterpart of a tape recording studio. These usually involve some additional hardware for high-speed recording and manipulation of the sound.

- **Other** categories of software are being dreamt up almost weekly, it seems. Some of these are totally new kinds of programs; others are crossbreeds of existing kinds (such as digital recording and sequencing, for the combined recording of sound and MIDI messages). As computer speed, memory, and processing capability increase, programmers are finding new things that can be done.

7

When Trouble Strikes

IT'S A FACT OF LIFE: The more pieces of equipment involved, the more numerous the connections, and the more controls that have to be set, the greater the likelihood that something will go wrong. Fortunately, problems with MIDI equipment are usually easy to locate, if you use your head and your ears.

There's an old story about a wealthy amateur musician who fancied himself to be a talented conductor. So he regularly hired an orchestra to play under his baton. On one such occasion, the timpanist mistook one of his wilder gestures for a cue and came in with a *brrrrrr-oom-boom!* The young man on the podium was furious. He silenced the music and in a loud voice demanded to know, "Who did that?"

You ought to be in a better position than that poor soul. When a problem occurs with your MIDI system, you should at least be able to eliminate some suspects by asking which unit isn't doing what you expect it to. Once you have done so, the next step is to define the problem. Exactly what is going wrong? From there you can use the table on the following pages to arrive at a solution. Most common MIDI problems are listed, along with their causes and suggested remedies.

Symptom	Cause	Solution
The instrument makes no sound.	Faulty or missing audio connections, or a level control turned down.	Check the audio connections and level settings. Make sure that a sound-generating program (patch) is selected.
The slave makes no sound.	Faulty or missing MIDI connections.	Connect a MIDI cable that you know to be good.
	Misconnected MIDI cable.	Connect OUT to IN or THRU to IN. Masters send messages from OUT, not THRU; slaves pass on messages via THRU, not OUT. If a sequencer is connected between the master and the slave, set its "soft thru" on, so that the OUT port acts as both OUT and THRU.
	Unit turned off upstream.	Turn on all units in a "daisy chain" (OUT to IN to THRU to IN to THRU to IN...) so messages flow to all units.
	Incorrect channel assignment.	Set the slave to receive on the same channel that the master is transmitting on.
The master makes no sound.	Local Control is off.	Set Local Control to on. Or, if connected to a sequencer, turn on the "soft thru" in the sequencer and connect the sequencer OUT back to the master IN.
One or more notes continues to sustain when it shouldn't.	The MIDI cable became disconnected before a Note Off message was received.	Turn off the instrument with the stuck note(s), wait a few seconds, then turn it back on.
	The MIDI transmit channel was changed before a Note Off message was received.	This will reset the unit and silence any hanging notes. As an alternative, some sequencers
	With sequencer playback: A Note Off message was erased during editing or re-recording into the sequencer.	and other devices feature a "MIDI panic button," which, when pressed, is designed to silence stuck notes.
	With sequencer playback: Playback was stopped before a Note Off message was sent.	
Slave produces additional notes it is not supposed to.	Omni is on.	Turn Omni off in slave that is to play only one channel of multichannel music.
	All parts are being played on one channel.	Play or sequence different parts on different channels.
Slave produces strange, non-tonal note patterns.	The drum machine (or drum track of the sequencer) is playing the slave.	Change receive channel on the slave or set the drum machine so that it does not transmit notes.

54

Symptom	Cause	Solution
Slave responds to some messages, but not to others.	Slave does not implement some messages.	Do without those messages, or use a different instrument.
	Transmission or reception of some messages is disabled.	Enable transmission and reception of all desired messages.
Fewer notes of polyphony are available on the master than normal. Tone color of sound is different than normal.	*MIDI echo.* The messages being sent OUT of the master are finding their way back to the IN, probably by way of the THRU of a connected instrument.	Turn Local Control off for the master. If this is not possible, eliminate the return path for MIDI messages. (If the master is connected to a sequencer, the return path may be via the OUT of the sequencer, if the "soft thru" function is on.)
Sequencer playback produces cacophony. Many more notes are being played than you expected.	*MIDI feedback.* The messages being sent OUT of the sequencer are finding their way back to the IN, and being sent out again and again by the "soft thru" function.	Eliminate one of the return paths for MIDI messages. If using a playback instrument, disconnect the THRU from the sequencer IN. If transferring information between two sequencers, turn off the "soft thru" function on at least one of them.
The sequencer or playback instrument locks up shortly after you begin sequencer playback. Some notes may be stuck on.		
The playback instrument displays an error message such as "MIDI Buffer Full."		
In transferring a sequence from one sequencer to another, lockup or errors occur.		
Drum machine and sequencer do not play in sync.	Both are using their internal clocks.	Set one to external (MIDI) clock, and connect it so that it is the slave of the unit that is set to internal clock.
Sequencer or drum machine does not run.	Unit is set to external (MIDI) clock, but no master unit is connected to it, or master unit has not been started.	Connect master unit to slave, and start and stop using the controls on the master unit. Or set the nonfunctioning unit to internal clock.
Slaves respond sluggishly.	Slow response of instrument to incoming MIDI messages.	Complain to the manufacturer. Use a different instrument. With sequencer playback, shift the track in question ahead by enough time to compensate for the delay, if possible.
Slaves in a "daisy chain" respond sluggishly or inaccurately.	Distortion of MIDI messages as they are passed from successive THRUs to INs.	Use a MIDI THRU box to connect multiple slaves to a sequencer or other master controller. As a quick fix, try changing the order of the slaves, placing the most temperamental ones nearest the master.

55

Symptom	Cause	Solution
Slaves respond sluggishly to sequencer.	*MIDI choke*. Too much information is being transmitted for accurate timing to be maintained.	Filter out unnecessary messages (such as after touch, pitch bend, or continuous controllers).
		Thin out continuous messages, if the sequencer offers this option.
		Use separate MIDI OUT ports for different groups of parts, if the sequencer has them.
		Synchronize playback of two sequencers, each playing some of the parts.
Sequencer memory runs out sooner than expected.	Too much information being recorded.	Filter out unnecessary messages (such as after touch, pitch bend, or velocity) on reception, or disable transmission of them by instruments.
		Thin out continuous messages, if the sequencer can do this.
The sound program used when recording a sequencer track is not the same one that sounds on playback.	Program Change message was not recorded as part of sequence.	Record the correct Program Change message at the beginning of the sequencer track, so that the program will be selected automatically when the sequence is played back.
A bass line was recorded into the sequencer using a bass program, and a rhythm part using a piano program, but they both play back using the piano program.	The instrument is not multitimbral; it will only produce one sound program at a time.	Use additional instruments to produce additional parts, or substitute a multitimbral instrument.
	The parts are recorded on the same MIDI channel.	Record different parts on different MIDI channels.
Sending a Program Change message calls up a different program than expected.	Program numbering is misleading on master, slave, or both.	Determine what program number is called up by what panel number. For example, program number 0 may be labeled 00, 1, or 11 on different equipment.
	Program changes are *remapped* on the master, the slave, or both. For example, when you select program 1 on the master, it might be set to transmit 5 instead. And the slave, upon receiving 5, might be set to select 19 instead!	Set the program map tables so that pressing the desired button calls up the desired program.
Sending a Program Change message causes the volume to jump.	The output level of the new sound program is not comparable to that of the previous one.	Program the desired output level or MIDI Volume setting into the slave as required. As a quick fix, use the volume control on the master or slave to change the volume level *after* sending the Program Change message.
	Some slaves, in response to Program Change messages, alter the MIDI Volume setting (Controller 7), too.	

56

Symptom	Cause	Solution
A controller produces a different effect than intended, or no effect at all.	The physical controllers on the master are not set to the MIDI controller numbers expected by the slave.	Change the controller assignment settings on the master, the slave, or both.
Instruments go out of tune when pitch bend is used.	Pitch bend range is set differently for the instruments.	Set the pitch bend range to the same value for all instruments concerned.
The pitch of an instrument has supposedly been transposed, but it still plays back sequenced music at the original pitch.	The transposition affects the pitch played from the instrument's own keyboard, and the MIDI messages the instrument transmits, but not the response to MIDI messages it receives.	Transpose the instrument before recording from it. If recording is already complete, transpose the sequence, if possible.
Some notes played by the sequencer are chopped short.	The total number of notes playing at a given time exceeds the available polyphony of the instrument(s) being used.	Reduce the number of notes playing at one time.
		Use sound programs or instruments that offer greater polyphony.
	The master controller generates All Notes Off messages, which are being recorded and played back.	Filter out the recording of the All Notes Off messages, if possible.
		Set the playback instrument(s) to ignore All Notes Off messages, if possible.

Grand Finale

IF YOU'VE READ THIS BOOK from cover to cover, you now know more about MIDI than most of the civilized world. And it wasn't so difficult to understand, was it?

But if you skipped ahead to see how the book ends, shame on you! Go to the chalkboard and write 100 times, "MIDI is our friend."

It turns out that the most complex thing about MIDI is the people that use it:

- There's the math genius, incessantly mumbling about "binary and hexadecimal numbering systems."

- There's the grammarian, unsure whether MIDI is a noun ("I'd like to buy a MIDI."), an adjective ("Is this a MIDI keyboard?"), or a verb ("I MIDI'd my system together last night.").

- There's the mystic, who sees in MIDI an allegory for the growing interconnectivity among people everywhere.

- And there's the ordinary musician or hobbyist, who recognizes that MIDI is a useful tool for making music.

No matter which of these categories describes you, MIDI is an interesting, exciting phenomenon. Enjoy it.

About the Author

JON EICHE has served as a writer and editor for Hal Leonard Publishing since 1980. In this capacity he has worked on owner's manuals and other books for Yamaha, Casio, Roland, Kurzweil, and numerous other manufacturers of electronic musical instruments. In 1987 he wrote the first book in this series, *What's a Synthesizer?* He frequently applies his knowledge of musical technology in performances at local churches with his wife, a singer.

He also moonlights as a music critic for the *Milwaukee Sentinel*, and has assembled and edited *The Bach Chaconne for Solo Violin: A Collection of Views* for the American String Teachers Association.

Index

Active Sensing, 39, 45
After-Touch. *See* Pressure
All Notes Off, 36, 45, 57
arpeggiator, 38
audio output, 11, 16, 18–19, 54
auxiliary messages, 45, 47
Basic channel, 36, 44, 46
byte, defined, 11. *See also* data
   byte, status byte
cable, 10, 54
channel messages, 13, 28–36
channel mode messages, 29,
   34–36, 44, 46
Channel Pressure. *See*
   Pressure
channel voice messages, 29–
   34
channelizer, 23, 49
channels, 13, 34, 56
clock, 38–39, 55. *See also* MIDI
   Timing Clock
computer, 20, 41, 50–52
Continue, 38, 40, 47
continuous messages, 32, 34,
   56
Control Change, 31–32, 44, 47

controller number, 32, 36, 56,
   57
daisy-chaining, 17–19, 54, 55
data byte, 12, 29, 30
delay device, MIDI, 38, 49
drum machine, 12, 37, 38–39,
   52, 54, 55
dump, 41
echo back. *See* soft thru
effects. *See* signal processing
errors, 19, 55
event editing, 21
expander module. *See* tone
   module
external (MIDI) clock. *See*
   clock
filter, 49, 56, 57
Global channel, 36
hardware, 9–10
ID. *See* manufacturer ID
imp chart, *See* MIDI
   Implementation Chart
internal clock. *See* clock
Key Pressure. *See* Pressure
layering, 16
lighting, 48

Local Control, 26–27, 36, 45,
   54, 55
lockup, 55
manufacturer ID, 41
mapping, 32, 33, 49, 56, 57
master controller, 17
master, 15–16, 38–39, 54, 55
merger, 25–26, 49
messages, 11–13, 21, 55
MIDI, defined, 8
MIDI choke, 56
MIDI echo, 55
MIDI feedback, 55
MIDI Implementation Chart,
   42–47
MIDI processors, 49
MIDI Time Code, 40, 41, 49
MIDI Timing Clock, 38, 39, 45
mixer, 18
mixing, 48
mode, MIDI. *See* channel
   mode messages
Mono, 34, 35, 36
monophonic. *See* polyphony
MTC. *See* MIDI Time Code
multi mode, 35
multitimbral, 24, 35, 56
music printing. *See* scoring
note number, 29, 44, 46, 57
Note Off, 30, 44, 47, 54
Note On, 12, 28, 29–30, 44, 47
Omni, 34, 35, 54
"panic button," 36, 39, 54
parameters. *See* settings
patch bay, MIDI, 49
Patch Select. *See* Program
   Change
patch thru. *See* soft thru
performance, 14–20

piano, 29
Pitch Bend, 33–34, 44, 47, 57
playback channel
   assignment, 23
player piano, 21–22, 29
Poly, 34, 35
polyphonic. *See* polyphony
polyphony, 34, 35, 55, 57
portable keyboard, 17, 20
ports, 9, 50, 54, 56
Pressure, 31, 44, 47
program, computer. *See*
   software
Program Change, 32–33, 45,
   47, 56
program number, 33, 56
quantization, 21
Quarter Frame, 40
rack-mount, 17
real-time recording, 21
receive channel, 13, 54
record channel assignment,
   23
recording, digital, 41, 52
recording, MIDI. *See*
   sequencing
recording, tape, 20–21, 49, 52
release velocity, 30. *See also*
   velocity
routing box. *See* patch bay
rules, MIDI, 11, 12, 46
running status, 30
Sample Dump Standard, 41,
   51
sampler. *See* sampling
sampling, 20, 41, 51
scoring, 52
sequence. *See* sequencing
sequencer. *See* sequencing

sequencing, 20–27, 48, 52, 54, 55, 56, 57

settings, programmable and non-, 13, 33, 34, 36, 41, 46, 47, 51, 52, 54–57

signal processing, 48, 49

slave, 15–16, 38–39, 54, 55

soft thru, 25–26, 54, 55

software, 20, 41, 50–52

Song Position Pointer, 40, 45

Song Select, 40, 45

stacking. *See* layering

star connection, 20

Start, 38, 47, 55

status byte, 12, 28, 29, 30, 34

step-time recording, 21

Stop, 38, 47, 55

stuck notes, 36, 39, 54, 55

synchronization, 38–39, 40, 49, 55, 56

synthesizer, 17, 20, 26, 31, 33, 39, 40, 51

sys-ex. *See* system exclusive messages

system common messages, 37, 40, 45, 47

system exclusive messages, 37, 41, 45, 47, 51

system messages, 13, 37–41

system real-time messages, 37, 38–39, 45, 47, 49

System Reset, 39, 45

theater organ, 14–15

thinning messages, 56

THRU box, 19–20, 49, 55

tone module, 16–17

transmit channel, 13, 23, 54

transpose, 46, 57

Tune Request, 40, 45

velocity, 29–30, 44, 47

volume, 29, 32, 56

What's a Sequencer?, 27

What's a Synthesizer?, 59

"Y" cord, 19, 25

YOUR ANSWERS TO UNDERSTANDING THE NEW MUSIC TECHNOLOGY

MIDI

WHAT'S MIDI?
Making Musical Instruments Work Together
By Jon F. Eiche

You've heard about MIDI and all the wonderful things it can do, but what is it *really*? What does it do, how can *you* use it in your music and where did that name come from, anyway? This book is the starting place for your journey into MIDI. It will answer your questions and then some. It keeps things simple, but doesn't skip over the essentials. If you've got MIDI questions, this book could be the answer you've been looking for!

00330044 $5.95

SEQUENCER

WHAT'S A SEQUENCER?
A Basic Guide To Their Features And Use
By Greg R. Starr

Sequencers are becoming a fact of life in today's music scene and with this book you'll see how they can work for you. If you own a sequencer, this book will cover both the basics of using it and the more advanced features of some models. If you don't have a sequencer but are thinking of buying one, you'll find enough information here to ask the right questions and decide which model is the right one for your particular needs.

00330045 $5.95

SAMPLER

WHAT'S A SAMPLER?
A Basic Guide To The World Of Digital Sampling

By Freff

You've heard the results in recordings, movie scores and TV commercials...sounds so realistic you'd swear they were the real thing - yet they're not. Welcome to the world of digital sampling! This book is your roadmap to finding your way around the basics of sampling - from definitions to how to make and use samples. Whether you're serious about sampling or merely curious, this book is for you.

00330004 $5.95

SYNTHESIZER

WHAT'S A SYNTHESIZER?
Simple Answers To Common Questions About The New Musical Technology
By Jon F. Eiche

Confused by the rapid pace of music technology, and perhaps a little threatened by it all? Relax. This book will explain, simply and briefly, the whats, hows, and whys of it all. You'll be provided with a basic grasp of the most important equipment and concepts, and then if you decide you want to know more, you'll be in a position to ask educated questions and understand the answers!

00183855 $5.95

For more information, see your local music dealer, or write to:

HLP Hal Leonard Publishing Corporation

P.O. Box 13819 Milwaukee, Wisconsin 53213

Prices & availability subject to change.